love
that hair

FOR AUDREY AND AGNES

AN HACHETTE UK COMPANY
WWW.HACHETTE.CO.UK

FIRST PUBLISHED IN GREAT BRITAIN IN 2017 BY ILEX,
A DIVISION OF OCTOPUS PUBLISHING GROUP LTD
CARMELITE HOUSE, 50 VICTORIA EMBANKMENT, LONDON EC4Y 0DZ
WWW.OCTOPUSBOOKS.CO.UK
WWW.OCTOPUSBOOKSUSA.COM

DESIGN, LAYOUT, AND TEXT COPYRIGHT © OCTOPUS PUBLISHING GROUP LIMITED 2017
ILLUSTRATIONS COPYRIGHT © EMMA LEONARD 2017

DISTRIBUTED IN THE US BY HACHETTE BOOK GROUP
1290 AVENUE OF THE AMERICAS, 4TH AND 5TH FLOORS, NEW YORK, NY 10104

DISTRIBUTED IN CANADA BY CANADIAN MANDA GROUP
664 ANNETTE ST., TORONTO, ONTARIO, CANADA M6S 2C8

PUBLISHER: ROLY ALLEN
EDITORIAL DIRECTOR: ZARA LARCOMBE
MANAGING SPECIALIST EDITOR: FRANK GALLAUGHER
EDITOR: RACHEL SILVERLIGHT
ADMIN ASSISTANT: SARAH VAUGHAN
ART DIRECTOR: JULIE WEIR
DESIGNER: LOUISE EVANS
PRODUCTION CONTROLLER: SARAH KULASEK-BOYD

LEMONBERRY SANS FONT USED COURTESY OF SABRINA SCHLEIGER
WWW.MONKEYROODLESFONTS.COM

FREELAND FONT USED COURTESY OF LAURA CONDOURIS
WWW.TRIALBYCUPCAKES.COM

ISBN 978-1-78157-497-3

A CIP CATALOGUE RECORD FOR THIS BOOK IS AVAILABLE FROM THE BRITISH LIBRARY.

PRINTED AND BOUND IN CHINA

10 9 8 7 6 5 4 3 2 1

love that hair

HEAD-TURNING STYLES FOR EVERY OCCASION

HAIR BY HAYLEY MALLINDER, ILLUSTRATIONS BY EMMA LEONARD

ilex

contents

hair 101

Ever see someone with a beautiful hairstyle on the street, catwalk, or in a magazine and get hair envy, wondering how they did it? I've been in the hair industry for a long time and often my clients say they have trouble styling their hair at home. They would also love the confidence to wear their hair a different way, if only they knew how.

The secret is to get to know your hair. Identify the type of hair you have and experiment with some good-quality products. Your hairstylist can help you with this.

In this book I've chosen 32 styles, beautifully illustrated by Emma, for you to try out. We start with some really quick everyday 'dos and work up to styles that are more intricate and time-consuming, suitable for a special event or a party.

Styling hair takes practice, but take your time and try doing it with friends until you've got the hang of it. You'll soon be adapting and combining the styles, and I hope this beautiful book will help you wear your hair a little different every day.

HAPPY STYLING!

Hayley Mallinder
& Emma Leonard

Haircare

Here are a few tips to help you keep your hair looking its best.

* Find a hairdresser you like and book in for a trim as often as you can manage (I recommend every 6–8 weeks), even if you are growing your hair. Regular trims help your hair maintain its shape and will stop it splitting.

* Never brush your hair when it's wet— it causes breakage. Spritz some leave-in conditioner through the ends of wet hair and work from the ends to the roots with a wide-toothed comb.

* Invest in quality hair products. They last longer and the results are far better. Ask your hairdresser's advice if you're not sure what's right for your hair.

* Use a professional-quality hairdryer if you can. They are more expensive but last a long time, give better results, and cut down drying time.

* Always use protective spray before using heat on your hair. When drying it, keep the temperature low, especially if your hair is fine-textured. Coarser hair textures can take a higher heat. Give your hair a break from heat styling—don't use heat appliances every day, and pop a treatment or moisture mask on once a week.

* Be cautious when it comes to big color changes. Always ask advice from a specialist and never attempt it at home.

Keep this up and you'll soon start noticing how much healthier your hair feels!

PARTS OF THE HEAD

1. Hairline
2. Top section
3. Crown
4. Nape
5. Middle of the ear
6. Back section
7. Temple area

Products & Tools

STYLING
* Leave-in conditioning spray
* Surf spray
* Thickening spray
* Thickening mousse
* Gel spray
* Hair-styling crème
* Curly-hair moisturiser or foam
* Hair oil

For Afro hair textures:
* Foam or setting lotion for wrapping
* Blow dry straight crème
* Heat protector

FINISHING
* Dry shampoo
* Texture spray
* Hairspray
* Gloss/serum
* Wax
* Hair powder
* Shine spray

TOOLS

* Wide-toothed comb
* Tail comb
* Grooming brush for updos
* Round brush for volume blowdries
* Cushion brush for straight blowdries
* Water spray bottle
* Section clips
* Grips (Japanese grips are best if you have Asian hair and are available online)
* U-pins or fringe pins (you can buy them all in one box called a session kit)
* Small hair bands (snag-free) for intricate braids and fine hair

* Medium hair bands
* Thick hair bands (ones without metal)

ADDITIONAL ACCESSORIES

* Crochet needle for hair sewing
* Wool
* Brooches or old earrings (to jazz up your braid)
* Tie-in glitter threads (great for festival hair or special events)

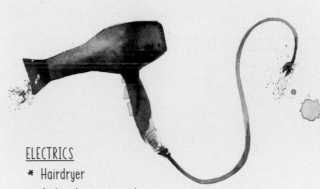

ELECTRICS

* Hairdryer
* Curling tong or wand
* Hair straighteners
* Hood dryer, if you have Afro hair, for wrap
* Diffuser

Tips for all textures

FINE

Help your fine hair get some body by using a thickening product like volume mousse or a thickening spray. Work some into the root area and use your fingers to give some lift before blowdrying. Next-day hair is easier to work with if you're doing an up-style. Apply a little hair powder for root lift and texture before you start. You can add in a few hair extensions to bulk out ponies and braids if you like.

COARSE

This hair texture can be difficult to work with since it can get very frizzy. Apply oil and a conditioning straightening or smoothing crème before blowdrying, and start drying your hair while it's still quite wet for a smoother finish.

STRAIGHT

Straight hair may have difficulty holding a curl, so use a product like a strong-hold styling crème or mousse to help it out. Thermoactive setting lotions are great to spray onto dry hair before using tongs. Clip each curl up while you finish the rest if your hair drops quickly.

WAVY/CURLY

Dryness can be a problem for these hair types so it's important keep your locks well moisturised with oil and a curl foam or crème. Always air-dry or use a diffuser if you want to keep your natural curls.

If blowdrying for a sleeker look, use a good smoothing or straightening crème and apply some oil. Hair at the front can be extra curly so start here first and blowdry in the direction needed for the hairstyle (e.g. for a ponytail, blowdry it back from the face using your cushion brush) and use hair straighteners for extra help.

AFRO

If you have access to a hood dryer, the wrapping technique is ideal for smoothing this texture to prepare it for styling, but a good blowdry helped out with hair straighteners works too. Don't overdo it with the straighteners though, as Afro hair is prone to breakage. Chopstick sets are a great way to get super defined, awesome-looking curls.

ASIAN HAIR

This type of hair can be heavy so some of the styles may need some extra securing. In the styles where small elastics are used for small braids, etc., use two or three just in case one breaks. For ponies buy extra thick elastic bands and look for some really strong grips online.

get up &

No more bad hair days, and no more boring 'dos! These styles are high-impact and low-maintenance, so get up and get styling!

side-twisted bun

1. Spray hair with dry shampoo or add hair powder to create texture, then tie a low pony slightly to one side.

2. Start twisting the hair.

3. Twist the hair up and around into a bun, and grip.

4. Wrap the tail of the twist around the base of the bun and grip. Let any loose strands fall naturally and the pull bun out to soften the effect.

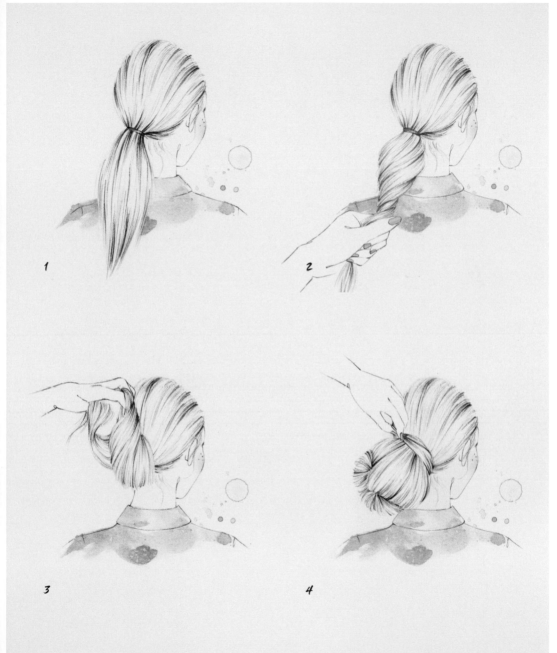

1

2

3

4

mop top knot

1

2

3

4

1. Put your hair up into a messy high pony and tie with elastic, letting a few strands come loose.

2. Backcomb the pony and apply styling powder or dry shampoo to give texture.

3–4. Arrange the bun around the elastic, keeping the texture soft, and grip. Pull it out a little to soften it even more, and spray with hairspray.

1. Part freshly washed hair on the extreme right or left.

2. Apply thickening spray or mousse and work through the hair. When the hair is roughly dried, smooth the top layers with a hairdryer and round brush. As you dry, make sure to work from the crown forward and slightly to the side.

3. Make a triangular section from the crown forward, with the point at the crown, and section away. Put the rest of hair back in a low pony and tie with elastic. Wrap a small piece of hair around the pony to hide the elastic, and grip.

(Continued on the next page.)

hideaway bangs

+ Work your bangs into the rest of your hairstyle and completely change your look!

4

5

6

4. Arrange the triangular section loosely over the ear, making sure your bangs are hidden under the upper layers and pushed to the side. Curl the middle section with curling tongs.

5. Spray with texture spray or dry shampoo, smoothing the front with a fine-toothed comb.

6. Pinch with fingers and separate the curls for a messy, textured look.

beach waves

+ Prepping your hair with surf spray will give it a perfect, lasting beach babe texture.

4

1

2

1. Work in small sections, one at a time, with the rest of your hair clipped out of the way. Leaving the roots straight, wrap the hair around a curling tong or wand. Start from the middle of the hair and wind almost to the end. Keep hold of the ends so they stay straight.

2. Continue this process around the whole head. If your hair has a natural wave, leave some of the natural hair out to add more texture.

3. Spray dry shampoo into the roots to give lift.

4. Shake your hair out to create a messy feel.

3

let it flow

soft bubble pony

1

1. Add powder or spray dry shampoo into the roots and backcomb through the crown.

2. Smooth the top layer of hair while keeping a bit of volume and softness. Tie into a low pony, allowing a few pieces of hair to fall down around the face.

3. Tie another piece of elastic a quarter of the way down the pony.

(Continued on the next page.)

2

3

4. Divide the loose end of the pony into two sections. Take a small piece from the left section to the right section, then take a small piece over from the right to the left. Repeat until halfway down the pony, then tie with elastic.

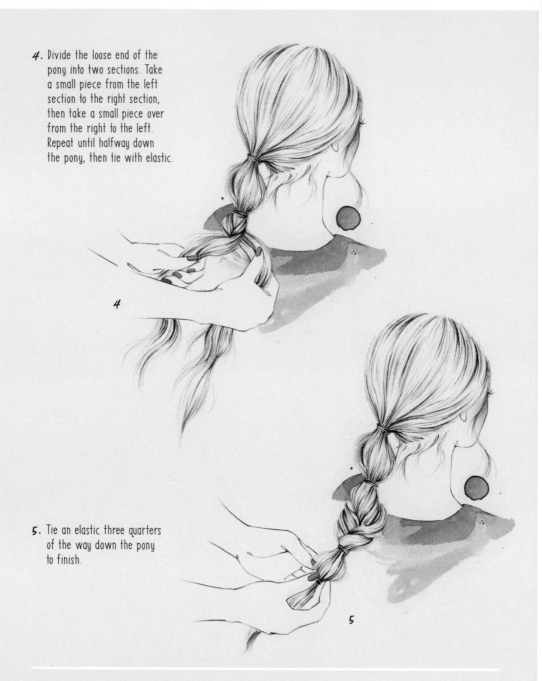

5. Tie an elastic three quarters of the way down the pony to finish.

chignon

1. Prep the hair with gel spray and tie hair in a smooth high pony.

2. Wrap a section of hair around the pony to neatly hide the elastic.

3–4. Fold hair forward and wrap around your finger forming a small, hollow bun. Spray with gel spray as you go and secure with grips.

+ Spritz with spray shine for maximum gloss!

1

2

3

4

work

& p

All work and no play is no fun for anyone! Here are some hard-working styles that don't take too much time to do and will see you through the whole day from morning to night.

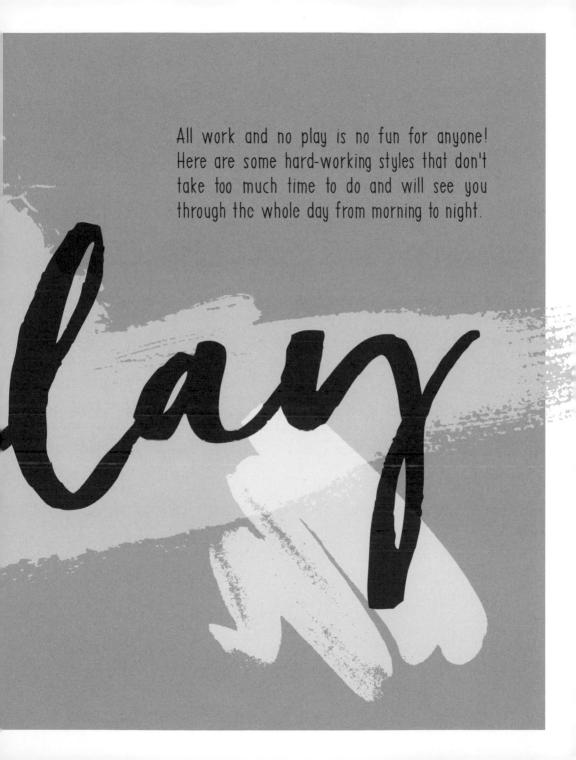

Rock 'n' Roll Twist

1. Backcomb the hair, especially at the crown. Apply hair powder and surf spray.

2. Keeping some height at the crown, pull the hair to one side.

3. Fold the hair over your finger, twist upward, and grip.

4. Loosen the sides over the ears and spray with hairspray to hold in place.

1

2

3

4

1. Separate the front of your hair from the back (use the middle of your ear as a guide). Tie the back section into a ponytail. Wrap a small section of hair around the pony to hide the elastic.

2–3. Roll the pony upward around your fingers to form the croissant and grip in place.

4–5. Take one half of the front section, split it into three pieces and make a basic braid. Tie the end with elastic, pull to the opposite side of the roll, and grip.

(Continued on the next page.)

le croissant

A super-chic style to pull out when you really want to impress!

5-6. Repeat on the other side so that the braids cross over each other.

Faux bob

1. Spritz washed or damp hair with surf spray to create texture and encourage a wave. Dry your hair with a hairdryer to activate the product.

2. Split your hair into two sections with a part in the middle and tie two loose ponies with elastic.

3–4. Tuck the pony under and pin at the nape with grips (use extra-strong ones, especially if you have thick hair). Cross the grips for a secure hold.

5. Making sure that the back is sitting neatly, arrange the front and sides to form a square bob shape. Pull out a tendril from the front to soften.

✚ Go from long to short without getting the chop!

WORK & PLAY

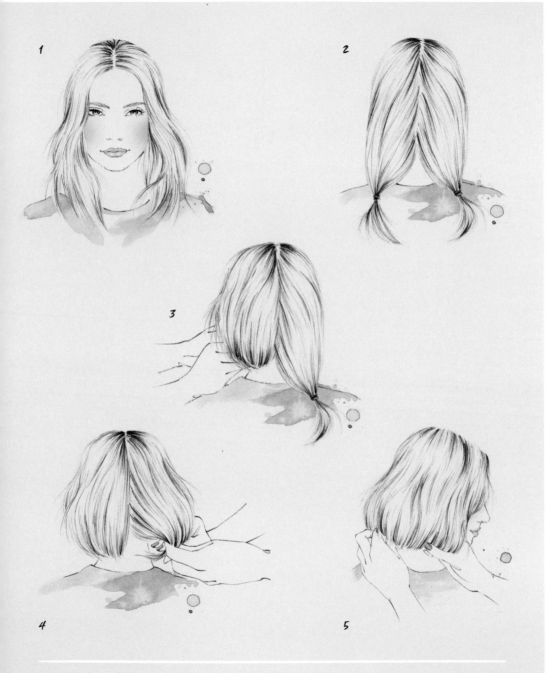

1

2

3

4

5

1. Apply curl- or styling crème and work into the hair.

2. Take two small sections from the front and side and tie in a loose knot.

3. Pick up another piece of hair from the top of the head and add to the left section. Tie another knot in the same direction as the previous knot.

4. Continue this pattern until you reach the back of the head or run out of hair and then tie with elastic.

5. Repeat steps 1–4 on the other side and connect the two together with elastic

Knotted halo

I am
effortless

dutch & french braid

+ Learn this basic braid and you can adapt it in any way you like. It's the starting point for several other styles in this book!

1

1. Take a triangular section from the front of the head, using the middle of the eyebrow as a guide for the size.

2. From this large section, take a smaller U-section in line with the nose and separate this into three sections.

3. Take the left section under the middle section.

4. Now take the right under, back to the middle.

(Continued on the next page.)

2

3

4

5

6

5. Now bring the left section to the middle again, this time adding a small section from the loose hair at the front-left of the head. Twist it under to the middle, and hold it in your left hand.

6. Repeat step 5, this time picking up hair from the right and combining with the right-hand section. Hold it in the right hand.

7 – 8. Repeat steps 5–6 all the way back until you reach the crown, then tie the end off with an elastic. Hide the elastic with a small piece of hair and grip in place.

9. Finally, separate the tail of the half-pony into three sections and plait it in a simple braid, left into the middle, then the right into the middle. Keep the braid loose and after you've tied it off pull out the sections to create big, soft loops (as on page 48).

+ The difference between a French and Dutch braid is that a French braid crosses the strands OVER the middle section, and the Dutch braid takes them UNDER. You've just learnt the Dutch braid.

7

8

1

2

sidewinder

1. Starting from one side of the head, take a section of hair and split it into three.

2. Start braiding around the head in a horizontal Dutch or French braid, adding hair from the top and bottom of the head as you work around.

3. Keep the braid going around the back of the head.

3

4. When you have braided as far across the head as you can go, curve around and braid downward until you run out of hair, and tie it off with elastic.

4

perfect
every
time

a new twi

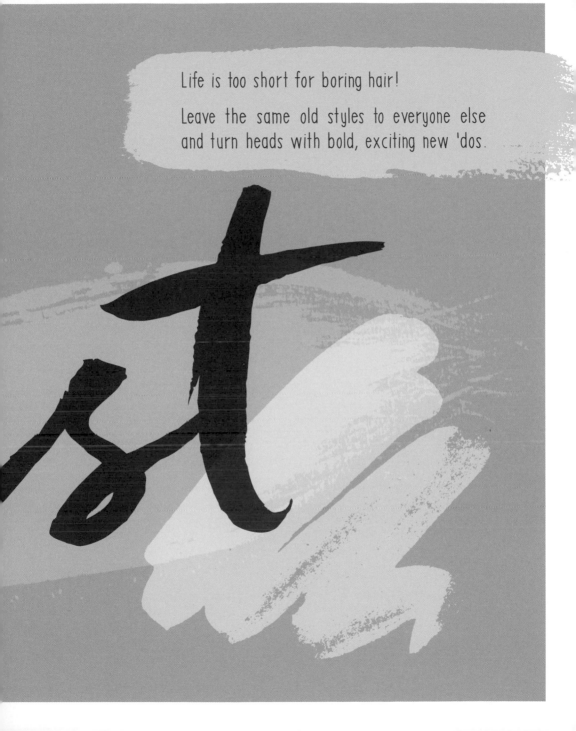

Life is too short for boring hair!

Leave the same old styles to everyone else and turn heads with bold, exciting new 'dos.

hyper bunches

1. Comb a section of hair at the top front of the head into a triangle shape. Tie the hair in an elastic band to make a small pony. Continue making triangular sections all around the head.

2–3. Take one of the ponies and separate it into two sections. Tie it in knots all the way to the end of the hair, wrap the ends under, and grip to hold.

(Continued on the next page.)

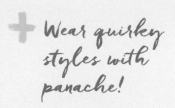 Wear quirky styles with panache!

1

2

3

4

4-6. Repeat steps 2-3 on all
the ponies.

5

6

7. Tie a small elastic over each
   bunch to secure.

7

1. Take a section of hair from both sides of the head just above the ear, gather the hair to the top, and put into a pony with elastic.

Next take a section from both sides of the head just behind the ear, gather to the middle of the head, and tie with elastic.

Gather the last section of hair and tie with elastic so you now have three centered ponies. Hide the elastic with a small piece from each of the ponies, and grip.

space princess

A NEW TWIST

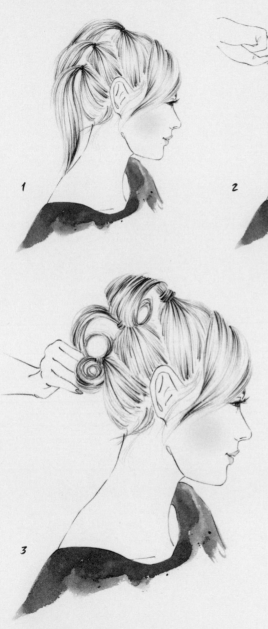

2–3. Starting from the end, roll each pony under and around your fingers and grip the roll firmly.

✚ Spray with hairspray for a polished look (and for extra hold at the party!)

1

2

1–2. Part the hair in the middle through to the nape of neck. Tie evenly spaced sections on both sides of the parting into ponytails, all the way from the top of the head to the nape. Tie the ponies on the back of the head, close to the center parting.

3–4. Join the first pony to the next one down, tying with a small elastic close to the elastic of the pony the first is piggybacking. Continue down the head until you have joined all ponies and repeat on the other side of the head.

dragon tails

3

4

5

5. Gently pull the sections apart to make a bubble shape.

your hair

your way

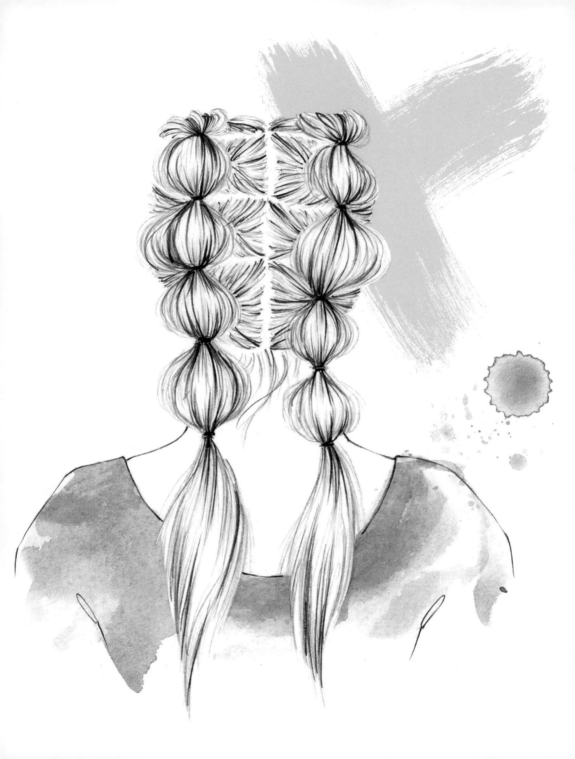

modern mermaid

1

2

1. Make a middle or a side part in the hair. Take a narrow section from the hairline to the nape and clip the rest of the hair out of the way.

3

2–3. Pull a small piece away from the rest, grip at the roots with the iron, and twist the iron downward. Hold for just a few seconds, then twist the iron upward, moving down the hair as you go.

4. Repeat this motion the length of the strand, keeping the movement flowing to achieve a soft look. Leave the ends straight for a modern look.

(Continued on the next page.)

4

5

6

5. Repeat steps 2–4 on a section beside the first. Follow this process the whole way around the head until you're ready to unclip the next section of hair.

6. Unclip another narrow section of hair above the first and repeat steps 2–5.

7. Repeat the whole process until all the hair has a wave pattern.

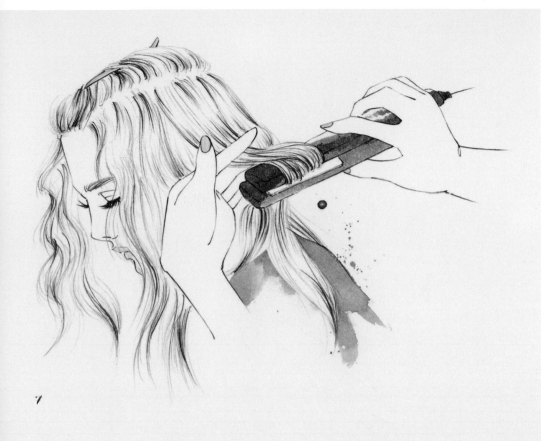

1

+ For a more natural look, drag your fingers through the hair to soften the curls and pull them out a little. Spray with hairspray to finish.

peekaboo braid

1—2. Starting at the crown, separate a section in the middle of the head, roughly a couple of inches wide, and section off the rest of the hair.

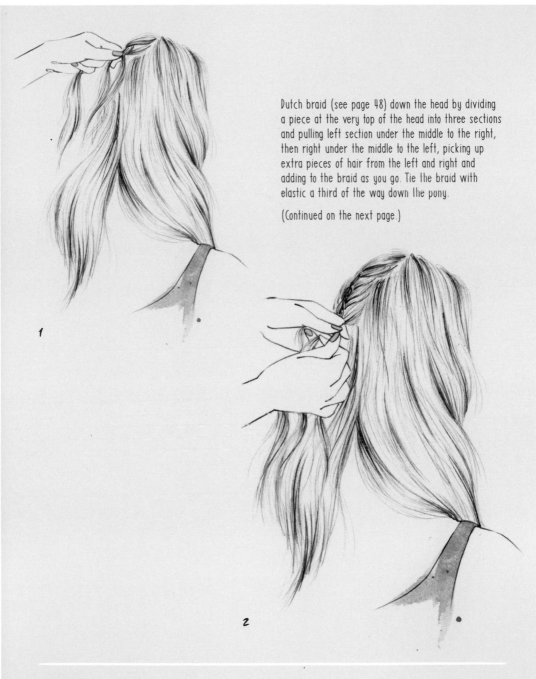

Dutch braid (see page 48) down the head by dividing a piece at the very top of the head into three sections and pulling left section under the middle to the right, then right under the middle to the left, picking up extra pieces of hair from the left and right and adding to the braid as you go. Tie the braid with elastic a third of the way down the pony.

(Continued on the next page.)

1

2

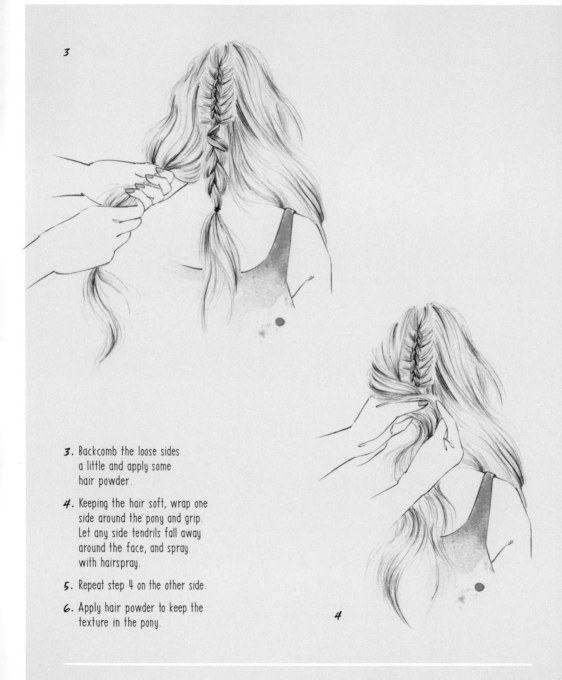

3

3. Backcomb the loose sides
   a little and apply some
   hair powder.

4. Keeping the hair soft, wrap one
   side around the pony and grip.
   Let any side tendrils fall away
   around the face, and spray
   with hairspray.

5. Repeat step 4 on the other side.

6. Apply hair powder to keep the
   texture in the pony.

4

5

A NEW TWIST

rope braid

1. Tie hair in a high pony. Wrap a piece of hair around the pony to hide the elastic, and grip.

2. Separate the pony into two sections. Twist both sections in a clockwise direction until you reach the end of each tail.

3–4. Making sure the twisted tails have a firm tension, wrap them around each other in an anticlockwise direction until you reach the end of the pony. Tie off with a small piece of elastic.

5. For a unique look, add vintage brooches, flowers, or anything else you like! (See overleaf.)

I am
unique

show pony

1

1. Separate a section of hair from the front of the head to the middle of the ears. Brush it back to the crown and tie it in a pony. Use gel spray to catch any flyaway hairs and to keep the hair smooth.

2. Tie some colored wool around the elastic and wrap around the pony until about three quarters of the way down, keeping the tension firm. Tie the wool in a double knot to secure, and trim off any ends.

3. Using gel spray to smooth, gather the rest of the hair into a low pony and tie with elastic. Tie the two ponies together with another elastic. Wrap some hair from the pony to hide the elastic and grip, or tie some more wool over the elastic for a neat finish.

2

3

step
out!

free spi

rit

These styles are made just for you!

Everyone has their own, unique style, and your hair can be part of that. Whether you're a rock chick, a bohemian beauty, or a bit of a princess, find your signature style here...

fishtail quiff

FREE SPIRIT

1. Take section of hair from the middle of the front of the head and separate it into two sections.

2. Take a small piece from the outer side of the left section, pull it to the right section, and combine. Then take a small piece from the outer side of the right section, pull to the left, and combine.

(Continued on the next page.)

3-4. Take a piece from the left, then pick up a piece of remaining hair, combine these two and pull across into the right section.

Repeat on the other side and continue until you reach the crown.

3

4

5-6. Push the braid forwards to form a quiff. Tie with an elastic.

Push some grips into the hair near the pony going forward to push the quiff out even more.

Wrap some hair around the pony to hide the elastic, and grip.

5

6

waterfall braids

+ Prep the hair by backcombing through the top, then smooth.

1

1. Take a section from the side of the head and split it into three. Take the left-hand piece over the middle to the right, then take the right over the middle to the left. Repeat, then drop the left piece.

2. Pick up a piece from the right to make three strands again. Take the right over the middle to the left, take the left over the middle to the right, repeat again, and drop the left section so two strands now hang free.

(Continued on the next page.)

2

3–4. Repeat the process in steps 1 and 2 all the way around the back of the head until you have four or five waterfall pieces hanging down.

5. Braid a little way down, then tie with elastic and grip under the hair.

3

4

5

+ If you wish, braid the waterfall pieces.
Backcomb the ends to hold, then pull out
and loosen the small braids slightly.

1. Make a parting along one side of the head down to the nape. If you have bangs, leave them loose. Clip the rest of the hair out of the way.

2. Make another small parting just above the hairline, curving around above the ear and down to the nape, leaving a narrow piece of hair loose. Clip the rest of the hair in the section out of the way for now.

3—4. Make a skinny Dutch or French braid (see page 48), beginning at the temple, close to the hairine, curving around the ear and ending the nape. Tie it off with a small elastic.

(Continued on the next page.)

1

2

sew into you

3

4

5

6

5–6. Unclip the rest of the hair in the section and start another skinny Dutch/French braid, picking up very small sections only from below, so that the braid stays close to the part. Continue down the head to the nape and tie it with a small elastic.

7. Using a large, blunt crocheting needle, thread colored wool under and over the braid to make a zigzag pattern. Continue threading until you reach the nape. Tie a knot to secure it in place and then trim the ends of the wool.

Loosen the rest of the hair and backcomb the crown a little to push it in a backward direction. Spray with hairspray.

7

Match the color
of the wool to
your outfit, your
accessories, or just
your mood!

express yourse

goddess hair

1—2. Part the hair in the middle of the head. Take a small, triangular section at the side of the part. Split into three and start a Dutch/French braid (see page 48), picking up hair only from the side nearest to the hairline (right hand if you're working the right-hand side of the face). Keep the braid tight and small, leaving a few tendrils loose around the face if you wish.

3. After you have braided about a third of the way down the strand, begin to curve around and start braiding back toward the crown. Now add hair to the braid from the top only. You can add quite large chunks to the braid as you work back.

(Continued on the next page.)

4. Braid to the end of the section and tie with an elastic.

5. Repeat the whole process on the other side of the head.

4

5

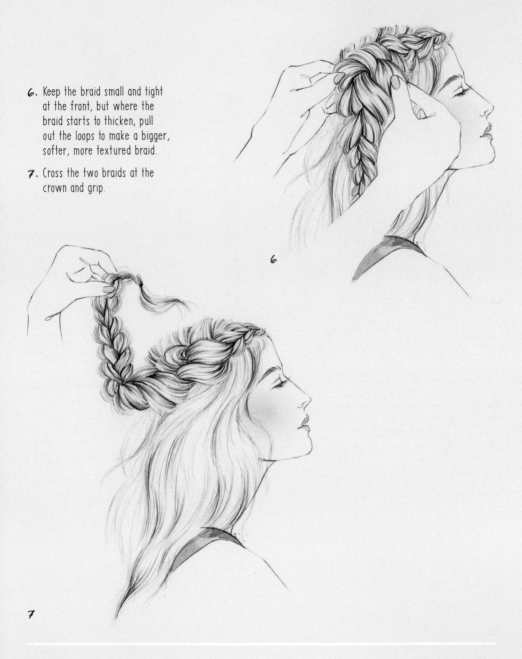

6. Keep the braid small and tight at the front, but where the braid starts to thicken, pull out the loops to make a bigger, softer, more textured braid.

7. Cross the two braids at the crown and grip.

6

7

Mohawk

1. Take a section of hair at the front of the head, tie it off and wrap a small piece of hair from the pony to hide the elastic. Use a tailcomb to loosen the front into a mini quiff.

2–4. Make a part across the head on either side of the pony. Begin a Dutch braid using the pony as the middle section. Pick up vertical sections from either side and add them to the braid right and left sections as you go. Make sure to keep the sides tight.

5. When you have reached the end, tie it with elastic, tuck it under and grip. Pull out and loosen the braid from the top for maximum volume. Keep the sides tight.

1

2

3

4

5

braided
headband

1

1. Separate out a medium-sized section of hair in the middle of the head, ear to ear. Clip the rest of the hair out of the way.

2. Take a piece of hair from the middle of the headband section and keep the rest of the section out of your way. Split the piece into three and make a skinny Dutch braid, starting from the top of the head working down to the ear, and picking up small pieces of hair from the path of the braid as you go.

(Continued on the next page.)

2

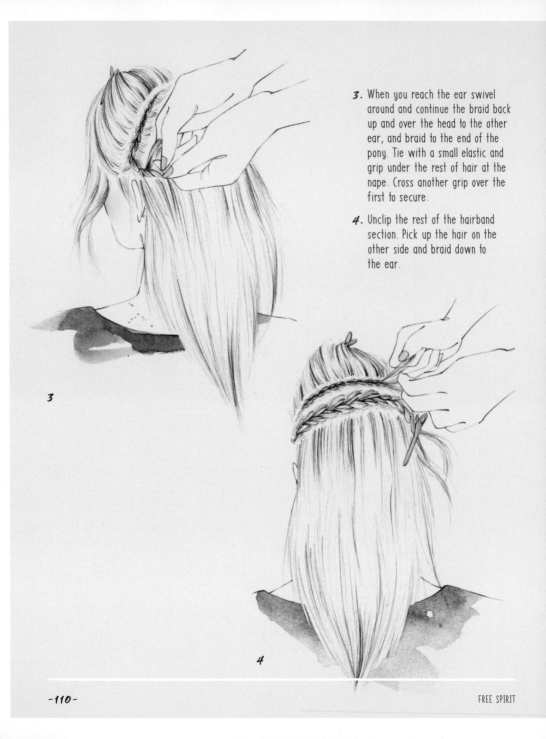

3. When you reach the ear swivel around and continue the braid back up and over the head to the other ear, and braid to the end of the pony. Tie with a small elastic and grip under the rest of hair at the nape. Cross another grip over the first to secure.

4. Unclip the rest of the hairband section. Pick up the hair on the other side and braid down to the ear.

3

4

5. Swivel around and braid back up the head to the other ear. Braid to the end of the pony and tie with elastic. Cross grips at the nape to secure.

6. Unclip the front and back sections of hair. Pull the front sections loosely to the back of the head and grip at the nape. Cross grips to secure.

5

disheveled
fishtail

1. Backcomb the crown then smooth over a little.

2. Take a section from the side of the head and split it into two.

(Continued on the next page.)

1

2

3. Take a piece of hair from the left section and pull it into the right section, and then take a piece of hair from the right section and add it to the left.

4-5. Add a piece from the rest of the hair to the left section, then pick up a small piece from the outer side of the left and take it to the right-hand section.

Now add a piece from the rest of the hair (from the front side) to the right-hand section. Take a small piece from the outer side to the left.

3

4

5

6. Continue across the head keeping hair loose. Let strands fall if they want to.

7. Keep braiding down the pony and tie with an elastic.

8. Pull the braid out a little to soften the effect.

life
of the

party

Sometimes you want to go the extra mile to stand out. When you need a style to make a splash, look no further than these head-turning 'dos!

1

1. Take a small piece of hair from the front of the head and tie with elastic into a pony. Wrap a piece of hair around the pony to hide the elastic, and grip.

Continue tying small sections into ponytails all the way down the head.

2—3. Split the first pony into two. Wrap the two pieces under the next pony and tie them with elastic. Take the next pony and do the same again.

(Continued on the next page.)

2

sailor's knot

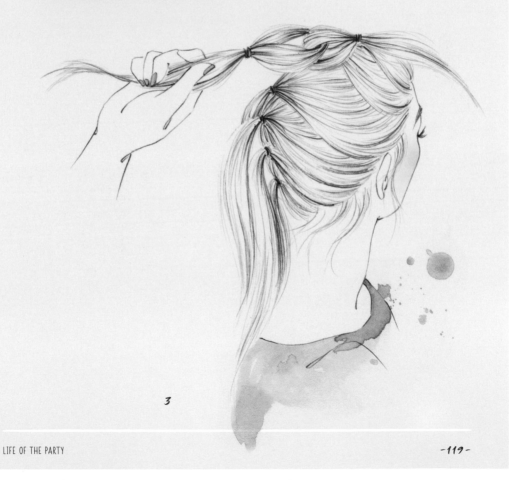

3

4. Keep dividing ponies into two and tying them under the next pony down, all the way to the bottom of the head.

5. Pull the loops apart to soften.

4

5

1. Make a part across the head, from ear to ear, to separate the front and back sections. Clip the back section out of the way for now. Using water spray, saturate the front section and push it out of the way.

2. Spray the back section with gel spray and comb through until extremely smooth, then tie back into a low pony.

3. Returning to the front, part the hair in the middle and apply strong-hold crème throughout.

(Continued on the next page.)

catwalk

4. Comb the hair forward and with a curve, preparing for the wave shape you're going to make.

5. Create the first wave by pinching the section into a small loop between your middle and index fingers. You can clip this in place if you need to.

6. Carefully comb the hair back and around, protecting the first wave with your middle finger.

7. Repeat steps 5–6 until you reach the hairline. Hold your waves in place, pinching to exaggerate the pattern, while you comb back the next bit of hair.

Comb the loose length of the front section back to the ponytail and twist it around the elastic tie, gripping to hold it in place.

8–9. Repeat steps 4–7 on the other side of the head, pinning the remaining hair around the pony.

4

5

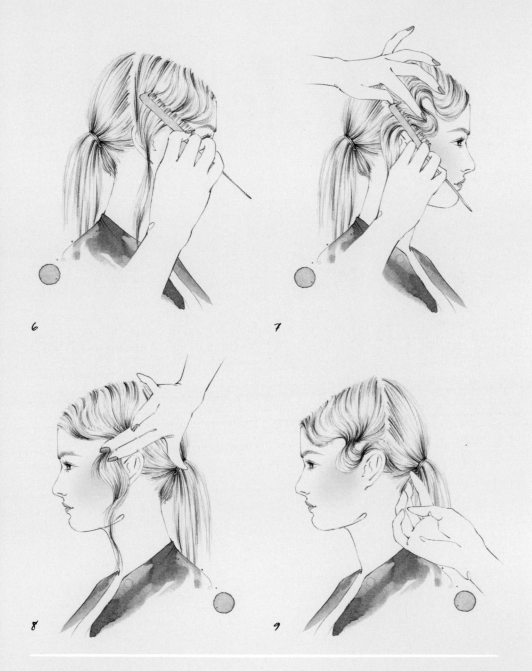

6

7

8

9

skullcap

1

1. Divide the hair on the top of
   the head into small, rectangular
   sections, tying each one in a
   small pony. Work in brick-like
   sections to the crown.

2–5. Separate the ponies into two
   smaller tails. Join one of the
   first-row half-ponies to one
   of the half-ponies directly
   behind it with an elastic band.
   Continue joining the ponies,
   working front to back, until
   you form a pattern and all of
   the half-ponies are connected.

   (Continued on the next page.)

2

3

4

5

6. Apply some moisturiser to the remaining hair to help separate the curls.

6

✚ This style is great if you have curly hair. If you do, give your curls definition with moisturising curl foam and oil before you begin. Let a few tendrils fall around the forehead.

LIFE OF THE PARTY

four-stranded braid

1

1. Part the hair down the middle of the head to divide it into two sections. Clip or tie one section out of the way for now.

   Take some of the side section and split it into four pieces. Let's number these pieces 1, 2, 3, and 4, starting from the left. Don't get too hung up on the numbers, though, because they will be changing!

2. Take piece 1 under piece 2, over piece 3 and under piece 4, and add a piece of hair from the side.

3. Piece 4 now comes back the other way. Imagine piece 1, which you've just taken under piece 4, is now called piece 3. So piece 4 comes over piece 3, under piece 2, and over the new piece 1—with which you now repeat step 2. Add a little piece of hair to piece 4.

   (Continued on the next page.)

2

3

✚ The four-stranded braid can be tricky until you get the hang of the pattern. Just keep practicing until it becomes fluid! It can also help to try it without adding extra hair, until your fingers remember the pattern.

4

5

6

4–6. Keep repeating steps 2–3. Remember, from the left: Under, over, under (swap), and add a bit of hair. And from the right: Over, under, over (swap), and add a bit of hair.

When there's no more hair to add to the braid, keep braiding a little way down the pony and tie off with elastic.

Now repeat Steps 2–6 on the other side of the head.

LIFE OF THE PARTY

7–8. Join the braids by tucking the ends under and securing with strong, crossed grips. Loosen the strands with your fingers.

7

8

practice makes perfect

gladiator

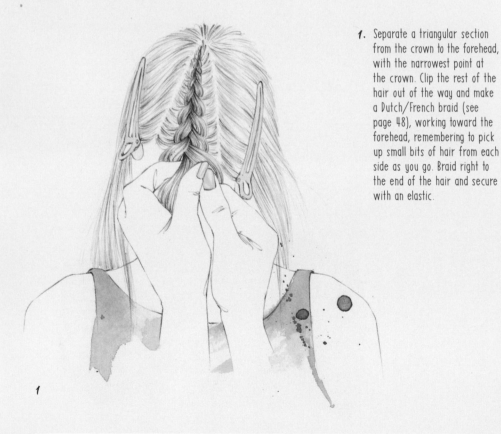

1. Separate a triangular section from the crown to the forehead, with the narrowest point at the crown. Clip the rest of the hair out of the way and make a Dutch/French braid (see page 48), working toward the forehead, remembering to pick up small bits of hair from each side as you go. Braid right to the end of the hair and secure with an elastic.

1

2 on the left, **3** on the right, above the illustration.

2. Fold the braid back on itself, tuck the tied-off end of it under, and secure with grips.

3. Now separate the remaining hair into two, with a clear part down the middle of the back of the head from the crown. Section off a piece of hair on either side of the braid, parting the hair along the side of the head, following its curve. Dutch braid these sections as you did for the top, but starting from the front of the head working toward the back. Keep working down the back of the head until you run out of hair to braid, then tie off with an elastic.

(Continued on the next page.)

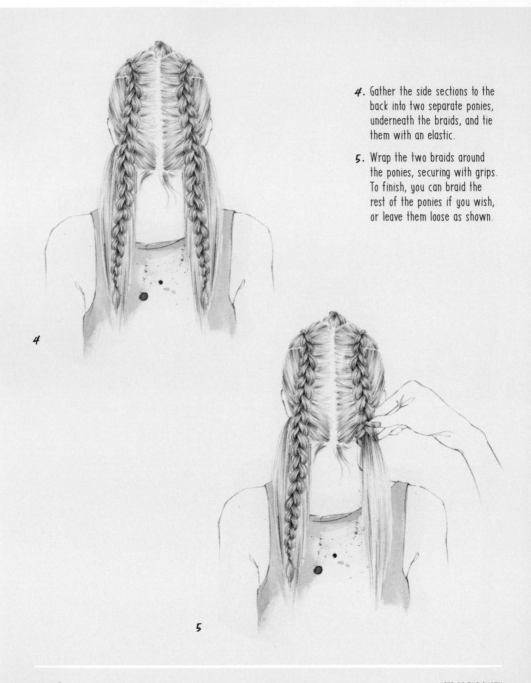

4. Gather the side sections to the back into two separate ponies, underneath the braids, and tie them with an elastic.

5. Wrap the two braids around the ponies, securing with grips. To finish, you can braid the rest of the ponies if you wish, or leave them loose as shown.

4

5

1

seashell

1. Take a small, circular section close to the hairline and separate into three small pieces. Start braiding around the front of the head, as if you are doing a Dutch or French braid (whichever you find easier), but taking hair only from the side nearest to the hairline. Make sure the braid follows a clear parting as you work around to the back of the head.

2. Clip the first braid in place for a while (or get someone to hold it for you) while you make a new circular section close to where the first braid ends. Join the first braid up with this section and continue braiding in a spiral pattern around the head.

3. Repeat step 2 to make a third braid. When you get to the back of the head, tie it off with an elastic and tuck it into a topknot, securing with grips.

2

3

good hair daze

ACKNOWLEDGMENTS
A special thank you to my workmates:
Patrick Matthews
Linzi King
Charlotte Cuoghi
Hermione Koutsoumanis
Rhiannon Taylor
Fleur Common
and the rest of the team at
Simon Webster Hair.

Thanks also to Seiko Yanagisawa.

Hayley Mallinder

Xo